It's hard, I know: Finding your balance

Leo D.Dennis

Table of contents

Chapter 1

Balancing a million aspects of life with 24 hours

If you are like most people reading this, I guess that you are quite busy. We are all really busy. Some of us even boast about it. But are you busy doing the things that truly matter to you?

The main questions are…
What does life balance mean? How do you perceive a balanced life? And most importantly, how do you go about attaining it in the middle of your insane schedule?

Self-discipline is one of the finest tools to help you get back on track and balance life. Without self-discipline, time is lost, you postpone, and you fail to follow through on things you know should be done.

You can adjust what isn't working for you and find equilibrium in your life. Remember that you do not have to alter everything at once. Making modest tweaks over time helps you identify what works best for you. Eventually, you will have a whole new set of beneficial living habits that will help you balance life.

So how do you start?

- Create a plan.

Create a strategy to go from where you are now to where you want to be. Maybe you need a new job. Maybe you need to go back to school. Maybe you need to deal with some relationship troubles. Whatever it is, build a strategy that will bring you to where you want to go.
I prefer listing my plan on a sticky note where I can see It.

- Focus on today.

Stop multitasking and concentrate on one thing at a time. It may be a project at work. It may be a talk with your closest buddy. It may simply be the book that you have wanted to write for months. The idea is to concentrate on one item at a time.

I plan each day the night before by choosing the three most critical things from my to-do list. In the morning I work on each one of these duties separately until they are accomplished. Once I accomplish these three activities I go on to answering phone calls, checking emails, etc.

- Just say no.

We all have too much to accomplish and too little time. The only way that you are going to find the time for the things that truly matter is to say no to the ones that don't. I utilize my purpose and life goal to make choices regarding the initiatives and things that I say yes to. If a project or assignment is not connected with my purpose, a good match with my life plan, and something that I have time to do, I say no to the endeavor.

Note that these three things should be part of what matters to you.
No compromise

1. **Your Health**

Your health does influence the quality of your life and work. Higher productivity and happiness reside in the balance of proper sleep, balanced nutrition, and physical exercise.
Your body is a fantastic sign when your life is out of control. One such indicator is low-quality sleep. Your overactive mind leads you to not sleep properly, and soon your energy levels plummet. Your mind seems fuzzy, and there appears to be disorder and congestion in your life.

If this seems similar, the best approach to take action is to seek methods to create space in your life and feel at peace.

Cultivate a Peaceful Mental State

Create mental space for peace: you can try utilizing an app for sleep and meditation. Make it a habit to meditate every day and utilize your selected app to help you remain committed.

Journaling

This is a simple habit that demands minimum effort. Journaling provides room in your head. Start by writing a single phrase a day to help you get started.

Eat Healthy & Exercise

A balanced diet generates natural energy and enhances your confidence and self-esteem. Exercise releases endorphins, which are the chemicals in our body that make us feel happy.

You may also book a consultation with a nutritionist to decide what healthy diet plan will work best for you.
Pick an activity that works for you: jogging, strength-training, yoga, pilates, walking, you have lots of alternatives!
Improving sleep, creating a peaceful mental space, having a nutritious diet and frequent exercise is the basis for preserving a well-balanced existence.

2. **Distance yourself from toxic individuals**

The idea is, to reduce the bad influences around you. This is crucial.
You may not realize how much these people's actions and words affect your life but believe me.

Avoid toxic individuals (complainers, whiners, lousy attitudes). If you can't avoid them, at least limit interaction and shut them out as much as you can. Surround yourself with encouraging, supportive, can-do individuals whenever possible.

3. **Spend Time Alone**

Making time for oneself is perhaps the toughest thing to accomplish for the normal busy and harried person, yet it is vital for decreasing stress, improving happiness, and stimulating creativity.

Some things to try: meditate, journal, draw, do some yoga or just sit quietly for a few minutes each day and do absolutely nothing.

Chapter 2

Balancing work without compromising personal time

Once upon a time, the borders between work and home were very apparent. Today, however, work is likely to intrude on your personal life, and preserving work-life balance is no easy undertaking.

Today's work life and hustle culture have us all seeking the best methods to manage our time, but let's be serious, there are only 24 hours in the day. All of us want to kill it at work, spend time with the people we love, and maybe even get a workout or two in. When our schedules are stretched to the fullest, you may wind up sacrificing the things that are essential to you. There is a lot of pressure to take that after-hours conference call and forego family supper. Or even forego your exercise so you can get a late-night work session in. This sort of forbearance might take a toll on your physical and emotional health. Living a fast-paced existence without any work-life balance encourages overstimulation and ultimately leads to disturbance in your personal life.

Sometimes it might even seem hard to be the ideal employee or business without jeopardizing your personal time. But, knowing how time management works helps you become a better worker even if it means having tighter availability and refusing last-minute jobs. When you learn to take control of your time you'll work smarter instead of harder. You create space to think clearly and creatively, so you don’t risk procrastinating. You’re also not hurrying to make hasty judgments. And lastly, when you preserve your time you’ll wind up getting more done and be a lot happier overall in life.

1. Set your daily agenda in advance. There's nothing more inhibiting than entering your day without an idea of where to start. Having no clear direction can lead you to feel overwhelmed. Right before your work day finishes, take the time each night to compose a to-do list for the next day. Prioritize your to-do list with significant chores, meetings, and crucial deadlines. This will help you feel secure about what to tackle first!

2. Know yourself and your productive hours. We can't all be early morning birds! Everyone has a specific period of the day in which they are the most productive at work; they are your peak hours. Self-assess and organize your work hours according to the time when you work best. If you can't choose your job hours, use this strategy for your passion project or favorite activity.

3. Cut out all distractions during work hours. If you want to be more effective at work, being focused will be key. You won't be able to work productively if your phone buzzes with social media alerts every five minutes. Mute all notifications and you'd be shocked how much you can get done without your phone giving you distractions.

4. Do the tasks that have deadlines first I know, we've all delayed that one terrible duty until we had no option but to take care of it. But postponing it will not assist with your work-life balance. Knowing you have to get it done eventually will simply drive you to worry and stress during your off hours until it's complete. So if you have a job that has a deadline, it's generally advisable to knock it done first!

5. Learn to delegate when required. Sometimes, we could take on more than we can manage. This is particularly true if you

are in a managerial role at work or you operate your own company. But delegating will keep you away from bad tension! If you don't want to work during your leisure time, trust someone else with a few chores. This will also enable you to concentrate on other elements of the work or organization that certainly deserve your attention too!

6. Take frequent breaks.

You don't want to exhaust yourself during work hours and end up too weary to enjoy the rest of the day. Regular 5 to 15-minute breaks help recharge your brain and enhance your productivity. There's a reason the Pomodoro method is so popular: taking pauses helps with time management. Breaks also assist to keep the creative juices flowing and prevent your energies from getting static! Choose your favorite interval and give it a try!

7. Use an app or project management tool to assist organize your time.

Some tools may help you manage all your key activities and to-do lists in one concentrated spot. You may manage both your professional and leisure time there, too. It's useful and you have it with you at all times. This will assist to guarantee you keep focused on what's essential and not spend any time on items that are not on your daily plan.

8. Plan each week.

It's usually a good idea to know what comes next, both with business and personal problems. Setting aside a little time each week to plan the following can help you arrange your time better. In this manner, you may attain a work-life balance without having to hurry to finish any crucial chores. Planning your week ahead of time is of course helpful for conference calls, meetings, and business initiatives. However is much more vital for personal care activities like fitness, facials, or massages. Plus of course helpful for arranging a social time with family and friends.

9. Set reasonable deadlines.
Don't commit to deadlines you know you won't be able to see through. This will only make you come off as untrustworthy with your colleagues. Plus you will feel stressed and exhausted. It's a pretty awful combo, right? Set yourself reasonable deadlines and commit to them.

10. Avoid multitasking tasks that require full attention.
Even while multitasking sounds like a wonderful idea to get a lot done, it implies some of the projects at hand are not receiving 100% of your attention or effort. When you multitask you are pushing your brain to overwork itself. This is a formula for exhaustion and human mistake. Switching

between things generates mental barriers that might slow you down! So for example, if you're working on emails simply concentrate on your inbox. Don't attempt to switch between emails and any other duties.

11. Choose when to multitask intelligently. Not all multitasking is bad. For example, sometimes is excellent to do something physical like going for a walk while you do something else that doesn't demand your legs or a ton of brain space. For example, maybe you go for a stroll outdoors as you catch up with a buddy over the phone. Or walk on the treadmill as you listen to your favorite podcast. You may even listen to your favorite podcast while in the shower or conducting a beauty regimen. This form of multitasking lets you achieve several activities that offer you delight and add value to your life.

12. Say no to what doesn't benefit you or your ambitions.
Being a people pleaser never helped anybody realize their ambitions or attain a good work-life balance. If you can't commit to that additional task, say no. If you need a Friday night to focus on your passion project, say no to that happy hour trip. Any work that doesn't seem right or makes you feel like you're putting something you truly want to complete on the back end, say no! When you put yourself first you will find yourself with a surprising amount of additional time. If you have a hard time saying no, check this article on how to create boundaries for additional inspiration.

13. Stay dedicated to your plan of action.
If you have a plan for your day, don't be disheartened by problems or subtleties that may come up. Stick to the timetable you have laid out for yourself! You will avoid

overworking yourself in an attempt to compensate for that time gap.

14. Automate as much as you can. Sometimes the tiniest of errands may throw you behind schedule and screw up your whole work-life balance. To enable yourself

time to concentrate on things of more value, attempt to automate things you don't need to take time out of your day to manage. For example, you may place your bills on auto-pay or have commonly used things like groceries and toiletries delivered right to your door. Automatization may save you plenty of time in the long run.

15. Don't wait for inspiration to hit. Effective time management is a skill that provides you the capacity to always be prepared and proactive. It keeps you from pushing inspiration or waiting for it to hit. If you are creative and you only work when

inspiration hits, then plan a specific time to think creatively. Schedule aside a block of time on the schedule to brainstorm. Delaying projects because you lack inspiration increases a bigger likelihood that you won't get it done at all, or anytime soon. Those jobs or projects will not complete themselves! Each time you put out effort towards your work, you're chipping away at it! Always show up for yourself, even on days you feel lethargic!

16. Get adequate sleep.
Coffee can't always be the miraculous cure for it all. Getting adequate sleep can help you feel refreshed throughout the day and be more effective at work. You'll be in a better mood too!

Chapter 3

Knowing your life is worth living

This makes organizing your life and establishing priorities simpler

You may have the sense of going home to your residence every night, eating the same cuisine every day, or conducting the same routines the following day.

It may leave you questioning if you are living a worthy life. Nobody knows how to perfectly live a worthwhile life since it is up to you and what worthy means to you.

And if it still feels like your life isn't worth living here are a few ways to stop feeling that way:

1. Do what you love
You only live once, so may as well live it by doing something that you love! There are instances when individuals find themselves in occupations they do not enjoy and did not choose. If you are in a scenario like that right now, then it may be better for you to search elsewhere.
Working in unfulfilling work is harmful and may lead to serious depression. Do not be frightened of what other people may think, take the chance, work hard, and do what you love!

2. Always strive for happiness.
Happiness is subjective. If dressed in full black makes you joyful, do it. If you performing volunteer work makes you happy, go for it. If possessing three bachelor's degrees makes you happy, try

hard to attain it. The main thing is to continuously strive for happiness!
Nobody wants to live an unpleasant life that is for sure. Although life may not always be sunshine and butterflies, if you constantly aspire for happiness, then you can always find the silver lining in any stormy weather.

3. Take inspiration from the world.
Do not enclose yourself within the four corners of your room. See the world outside and draw inspiration from it! Being open-minded helps a lot in these circumstances. If you are open to various types of ideas, then there might be greater potential for knowledge and progress.
If you can, you may also take a soul-searching tour across other nations and see many various cultures, meet all types of people, and get to know their unique tales. Knowing that there is so much more to the world than you know may even make you reflect on your own life.

4. Do something that you have always wanted to do.

Another method to make your life worth living is to do something that you have always wanted to do. Every day is a fantastic chance for you to tackle something that you have never done before! If you constantly perform the same thing every day, then it is sure to lose its significance, particularly if it is something you do not enjoy doing.

Take the step of bravery and try it out! It may be as fascinating as coloring your hair purple or taking tap dance courses. The essence of the matter is, that you will be able to discover things that you never considered or even dreamt of performing previously till now! This might also be a means for you to find yourself since as human beings, we never stop evolving.

5. Help people who are in need.
Be a volunteer for an organization, give your unwanted clothing, or feed the homeless, these are just three of the numerous activities that you can do to assist people who are in need. The world is full of heroes and you may always be one of them! You need not have superpowers, having a decent heart and functioning hands are all it takes to bring a smile to a person's face. Helping others may also be your advocacy in life, or in other words, it is what makes your life more fascinating and worth living.

6. Work with enthusiasm.
Whatever it is that you do, do it with full enthusiasm, because if you do, then you will never grow weary of doing it. Even the simplest job of sweeping the floor may be done with enthusiasm.

If you do your duty with enthusiasm, then it will not only be gratifying for you but also for people who are around you and experience the results of your efforts.

If you are a teacher, then make it your principle to properly educate the future of the country! Take your task to heart and it will always be successful in the end.

7. Do not be frightened to make errors.

Be a wise risk-taker! Do not be scared to make errors since we are just human. If you make a mistake, you should move on from it and use it as a lesson.

If you linger too much on the numerous errors that you have made in the past, then you will be entirely hung up over it and may even continue to do the same mistakes. You can be locked in a loop that never ends, a cycle filled with regret and anger. Allow oneself to be free to make flaws. The key thing is that you always remember to get back up anytime you fall.

8. Be the cause that someone smiles today. Seeing a person smile and knowing that you are the cause behind it, is one of the simplest things in life that make living worthwhile. It may be as easy as contacting your parents to tell them how much you love them, giving your niece a lollipop, or simply clapping your buddy on the back after he or she did a fantastic job on his assignment! Happiness is contagious therefore be sure to distribute it all around you, from the strangers you meet up to the ones you love.

9. Try trying various things.
If you never thought of yourself as someone who would go bungee jumping then maybe you should. Aside from doing things you have always wanted to do, you should also try out things that you never would have dreamed of doing! Sometimes following the path less traveled, may be extremely shocking but exciting since you never know where you could wind up.

If there is a call waiting for a job in a different location, why don't you attempt and accept it? Who knows you could even believe in the end that you genuinely enjoy it! Or if there is a meal that you would never eat then maybe it's time to test it out.

10. Live your life to its best extent.
Lastly, you should live your life to its maximum extent. Discover the globe and take chances! That is the only way to find out what you want to accomplish to make your life worth living. It may be a cliché, but it is a cliche for the reason that it is true and has worked many times before.
It is up to you to assess the merit of how you conduct your life. You may always settle for what is known and secure, although sometimes what is safe can also be what is uninteresting.

Human life is meant to be lived, so never waste the opportunity to discover new things, try out different foods, and experience unique events so that when you are gray and old, you will be able to look back at your life and truly say that it was all worth it.

Chapter 4

Maintaining your now balanced life

Ok so after following some or all steps in chapter 1 and now you feel a bit more balanced, how do you maintain this?

Have healthy self-esteem: this is so necessary. Good self-esteem won't let you break down when you see people doing so well on social media and even around you. Instead, it motivates you. It's hard to say don't compare yourself but minimize it, don't think too much about it.

Make friends that matter and give a damn about you: I'd rather have zero friends than have a bunch of friends who are shitty and just don't add any value to me.

So yea, that's pretty important, those friends are kind of like trackers. Those friends ask about your progress and genuinely want you to succeed.

Learn how to manage stress effectively: When you're starting to get a hold of your life, you might feel pressure to keep up, stress generally from sticking to your schedule, and work.
At this time, you can take a break from social media, and the news and just unwind in your way. Avoid alcohol when you're stressed though, you don't want that to be your go-to and get addicted.

Remember, you're just a human in the end:
Some people might think it's only work life that's stressful... How much more wrong can they be? Personal life and just dealing with family is a whole other world so chill. You're not a robot that just takes everything, don't be too hard on yourself.

Know when you need help:
As I said, you're not a robot. You might feel overwhelmed with work, plans, and schedules, or maybe you need someone to talk to.
Ask for help, it might be hard sometimes, but please do.

Final chapter

Your mental health and know when you need professional help.

You need personal time away from work and even other people in general. Sometimes, time alone is what you need to avoid popping open like a shaken up soda. I don't know if you understand, but when you feel too furious, or suffocated, just breathe. Taking "breathe" literally, helps significantly. You may do breathing exercises that take only a few minutes of your time.

Alone time also plays a key function in mental wellness. Being near other people comes with benefits, but it also produces tension. You worry about what others think. You adjust your conduct to escape rejection and to fit in with the rest of the group.

While it may be the cost of being part of a social environment, some of these problems highlight why alone time may be so crucial. Having time for yourself allows you the ability to break away from societal expectations and dig into your ideas, emotions, and experiences.

But being alone isn't always easy.
Alone time may be tough for some individuals for several reasons. One research indicated that many individuals would prefer to give themselves unpleasant electric shocks than merely sitting alone with their thoughts so…
There are a variety of reasons alone time might be problematic :

Lack of experience being alone: Some individuals simply may not be used to being by themselves since they are so used to being around other people. The abrupt lack

of social stimulation might leave them feeling distant or disconnected.
Distressing thoughts and feelings: In other instances, being alone and thinking inward might be difficult or even unpleasant. People could find this reflection disturbing or find themselves immersed in rumination and concern.

Social stigma: For people who have been exposed to unfavorable views about being alone or who regard it as a type of antisocial conduct or social rejection, isolation may appear like a painful sort of punishment.

Note: If your time alone makes things worse, please seek professional help.

www.ingramcontent.com/pod-product-compliance
Lightning Source LLC
LaVergne TN
LVHW020535160826
845677LV00015B/4079
* 9 7 9 8 3 5 1 6 7 9 9 3 8 *